VERMONT

in words and pictures

BY DENNIS B. FRADIN

ILLUSTRATIONS BY RICHARD WAHL

MAPS BY LEN W. MEENTS

Consultant:
Perry Hanson, III
Chairman, Department of Geography
Middlebury College
Middlebury, Vermont

 CHILDRENS PRESS ™

CHICAGO

To my aunt, Edith Cohen

West Dover

Picture Acknowledgments
COVER—Covered bridge in Grafton
VERMONT TRAVEL DIVISION—Cover, 2, 4, 8, 11, 17 (left),
23, 25, 28 (right), 30, 31, 34, 35, 36, 37, 38, 40, 43
KILLINGTON SKI RESORT—17 (above), 24, 28, 29
GREEN TRAILS INN, Brookfield—20, 21
UNIVERSITY OF VERMONT, Morgan Horse Farm
(Dr. Donald J. Balch)—33

10 11 R 93 92 91

Library of Congress Cataloging in Publication Data

Fradin, Dennis B.
  Vermont in words and pictures.

  SUMMARY: A brief introduction to the land,
history, cities, industries, and famous sites of
the Green Mountain State.
  1. Vermont—Juvenile literature. [1. Vermont]
I. Wahl, Richard, 1939-   II. Meents, Len W.
III. Title.
F49.3.F7   974.3   79-22069
ISBN 0-516-03946-6

Vermont (ver•MAHNT) comes from the two French words *Vert* (vairt) and *Mont* (mohn (t)). They mean Green Mountain. The Green Mountains run down the middle of Vermont like a backbone. Vermont is nicknamed the Green Mountain State.

Vermont is famed for its maple syrup and its fine granite and marble. The state is also famous for its strong-willed people.

Do you know what state the "Green Mountain Boys" came from? Do you know which state first banned slavery? Do you know where Presidents Arthur and Coolidge were born? Do you know where the first Boy Scout troop in America was formed? As you will learn, the answer to all these questions is—Vermont, the Green Mountain State.

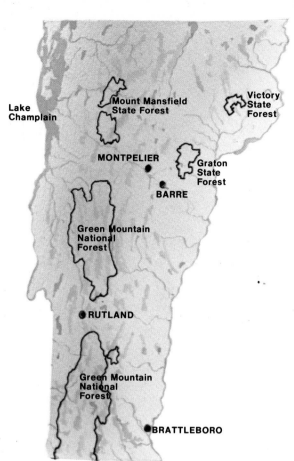

Glacial Lake, Willoughby

If you push the ends of a rug together, it will rise in the middle. In the same way the Green Mountains were folded up out of the earth, about 350 million years ago.

At one time much of Vermont was covered by water. How do scientists know? Fish fossils have been found on dry land. A whale's skeleton was found in Charlotte.

About a million years ago the Ice Age began. Huge mountains of ice, called *glaciers* (GLAY • sherz), covered

4

Vermont. Glaciers dug big holes in the ground. In time the glaciers melted. The holes filled with water, forming lakes and ponds.

People lived in Vermont at least 10,000 years ago. They made spears for hunting. They fished with nets. Some early people lived in caves. Some made paintings on cliffs that can still be seen today. Scientists are still digging to learn more about early Vermont people.

Modern Indians are related to these early people. Not many Indians made Vermont their home. Indians went to hunt in Vermont. They hunted deer and bears with bows and arrows. While hunting they lived in tepees. These were skin tents that could be moved from place to place. Indians built canoes. Indians tapped maple sap and made maple syrup.

Two Indian groups had hunting grounds in Vermont. The Algonquin (al • GONG • kwin) Indian family was first.

The Abnaki (ab • NAH • kee), Mahican (ma • HEE • kin), Pocumtuc (po • CUM • tuck), Coos (COOZ), and Penacook (PEN • ah • cook) were some tribes of the Algonquin Indians.

Iroquois (EER • ih • kwoi) Indian tribes came later. They came from the New York area. The Mohawk (MO • hawk), Seneca (SEHN • ih • ka), and Oneida (oh • NYE • dah) were three tribes of the Iroquois family.

Iroquois and Algonquin Indians were enemies. They fought fiercely.

The French were the first non-Indians in Vermont. In 1609 Samuel de Champlain (sham • PLANE) entered what is now Vermont. Some think there were other explorers before him. But Champlain is the first explorer *known* to have entered Vermont.

Champlain came down from Canada with two other Frenchmen and some Algonquin Indians. They paddled

24 canoes south on a large lake. Samuel de Champlain named it Lake Champlain—for himself.

The Frenchmen had guns. Near the banks of Lake Champlain they met some Iroquois. The Indians knew nothing about guns. They came closer, ready to attack. Champlain fired. One Iroquois chief was killed. He fired again. A second chief was wounded. Another Iroquois was shot by a Frenchman. Iroquois Indians were taken prisoner.

Lake Champlain

Champlain claimed the area of Vermont for France. He also started a long fight between Indians and white men.

French fur trappers came. They caught beaver and other furs that could be sold. French people were given land to farm. In 1666 Frenchmen built a fort on Isle La Motte (MOHT) in Lake Champlain. About 300 soldiers came to the fort to protect the few French settlers. Other French forts and settlements were built in the Lake Champlain area. The biggest French settlement was at Chimney Point. French priests also came. Their job was to teach the Indians about Christianity.

By the early 1700s, England ruled the 13 American colonies. England wanted Vermont, too. In 1724 the English built Fort Dummer near present-day Brattleboro (BRAT • el • burro). Fort Dummer is often called the first permanent white settlement in Vermont.

The Indians wanted the land. The French wanted the land. And the English wanted the land. They fought for almost 100 years over this land. This fight is called the French and Indian War. Algonquin Indians helped the French. Iroquois Indians helped the English.

Much blood was shed on all sides. Indians were shot. Indian villages were burned. Some settlers were killed. Others were captured by Indians. James and Elizabeth Johnson and their three children were captured. The Indians marched them through Vermont into Canada. On the trail in Vermont, Mrs. Johnson had a baby girl. She

named her "Captive." The Johnsons were held for four years. They were finally freed. Elizabeth Johnson lived to be 81. Captive, one of the first white children born in Vermont, lived to have her own family.

Major Robert Rogers helped the English. He led a group called Rogers' Rangers. Dressed in green deerskin, they fought the Indians who sided with the French. Rogers' Rangers destroyed an Indian village near the town of Swanton (SWAN • tun). Two hundred Indians were killed in this night raid.

The English General Jeffery Amherst (AM • herst) took French forts on Lake Champlain. By 1763, the English had won. The French and Indian War was over.

More settlers came to Vermont. Many came in wagons pulled by oxen. They cleared forests. They built log cabins. They farmed. Small towns like Westminster (WEST • min • ster), Bellows Falls, and Bennington were built.

Vermont was ruled by England. So were the 13 colonies. Two colonies—New Hampshire and New York—had both granted land to settlers in Vermont. Often, it was the same land. King George III of England

Weston

said that New York owned Vermont land. He said that people with New Hampshire land grants had to pay for their lands or get out.

Settlers were angry. They had built farms on this land. They had built towns. They didn't want to pay New York for the land. People with New Hampshire grants decided to fight the "Yorkers."

In 1770 Vermonters formed an army called the "Green Mountain Boys." They wanted to keep their land and push the New York settlers out of Vermont. The Green Mountain Boys met at the Catamount (CAT • ah • mount) Tavern in Bennington. A tall, strong farmer named Ethan Allen was their leader. Their other leaders were Ethan's brother Ira Allen and Ethan's cousins Seth Warner and Remember Baker.

The Green Mountain Boys burned the houses of Yorkers. They stole their cattle. They whipped New

York lawmakers with switches. Some Yorkers got the "high chair treatment." They were tied to a chair which was then raised high above the Catamount Tavern and left there. Many Yorkers were driven away. The Green Mountain Boys did not kill people, however. Because he protected the lands of the poor farmers, Ethan Allen was called the "Robin Hood of Vermont."

Something important stopped the fighting against the New Yorkers—the Revolutionary War.

Many people did not want to be ruled by England any longer. "We've built up this land ourselves!" said many Americans. "We don't want to pay taxes to England any longer." They decided to make a new country — the United States of America.

Fighting broke out in 1775. Vermont already had the Green Mountain Boys. They were ready to fight. Now the people from Vermont, New Hampshire, and New York battled a common enemy — the English.

The Green Mountain Boys met at the Catamount Tavern. They decided to capture Fort Ticonderoga (ty • kon • der • OH • gah) in New York. With Benedict Arnold's help, Ethan Allen and 83 of his men crossed Lake Champlain. Ethan Allen had never been inside the fort. A young boy named Nathan Beeman went with them. Nathan knew the fort. The Green Mountain Boys rushed the fort on May 10, 1775, in the middle of the

night. The English were sleeping. The English
commander was caught in his underwear.

"Surrender!" said Ethan Allen.

"In whose name?" asked the commander.

Ethan Allen then said these famous words. "In the
name of the great Jehovah and the Continental
Congress!" (The Continental Congress was the
forerunner of the United States Congress.)

No one was killed. No shots were fired. The Americans took 150 cannons from Fort Ticonderoga. Two days later, on May 12, 1775, Seth Warner took the English fort at Crown Point. The Americans held Fort Ticonderoga for two years. Then the English won it back.

The Battle of Hubbardton (HUH • bart • en) on July 7, 1777, was the only revolutionary battle actually fought in Vermont. Seth Warner and the Green Mountain Boys lost the battle. But Warner gave American troops time to escape from Fort Ticonderoga. One month later, on August 16, 1777, Seth Warner and General John Stark led the American troops at the Battle of Bennington in New York. This bloody battle was an important victory for the Americans. Ethan Allen was not at this battle. He had been captured and was in jail in England.

Above: Killington Peak. Troops marched past this
peak on their way to the Battle of Bennington.
Left: Statue of Seth Warner in Bennington

England was finally beaten. The Revolutionary War
ended in 1783. A new country had been born—the United
States of America.

After the war Vermonters were still fighting about
land. For years Vermont was an independent republic.
At first it was called *New Connecticut*. Then Dr. Thomas
Young suggested the name *Vermont*. Finally, Vermont
and New York ended their fight. Vermont gave New
York $30,000 to pay for the land.

On March 4, 1791, Vermont became America's fourteenth state. It was the first state to enter the United States after the first 13 colonies. It was also the first state to ban slavery in its state constitution. The first governor of Vermont was "One-eyed" Thomas Chittenden (CHIT • en • dun). He was governor for 18 years. Montpelier (mont • PEEL • yer) became the state capital in 1805.

People poured into Vermont. They came to farm. Between 1790 and 1810 the number of people in Vermont grew from about 85,000 to about 218,000.

Life was hard. The people grew corn. They hunted deer for meat. Milk came from their own cows. The settlers built churches and schools. In those days, children going to school had to watch for wolves and bears. Schoolchildren wrote with goose quill pens—if they had paper.

In the spring, children helped plant crops and build fences. In the summer they helped tend the livestock. In the fall they harvested the crops.

The people had fun, too. After the corn was picked, people gathered for cornhusking bees. Fall was also a time for a Thanksgiving feast—if the crops had been good. In the winter, people had "sugaring-down" parties. Adults boiled the maple sap into syrup. Children poured boiling syrup on snow to make a candy known as "sugar-on-snow."

Ethan Allen got out of the English jail in 1778. He returned to America. He was sick and very thin. But he was a hero. Some called him the "Father of Vermont."

Horse-drawn sleigh, Brookfield

Like other pioneers, Vermont people liked to tell "tall tales." Vermont has short summers and long, cold winters with deep snow. According to one tall tale, old people in Vermont were frozen in the winter. They were kept in a block of ice and snow. At about corn-planting time, the ice was chopped away. The people awoke, refreshed and ready for spring!

In 1816 people wished they really *could* sleep through the cold weather. That year a foot of snow fell in June. Snow fell in July and August, too. Crops withered. Livestock died. Vermonters called 1816 the "Starvation Year" and the "Year Without a Summer."

Floating Bridge, Brookfield

At last the winter ended. Some Vermonters sold their farms and moved west. But most refused to leave. No other winter in Vermont has ever been *that* bad.

During the 1820s and 1830s, many Vermont farmers raised Merino sheep. Wool from these sheep made warm clothes. The Champlain Canal opened in 1823. Farmers now could send wool and other goods by boat to New York City.

By the time of the Civil War the sheep industry was ending. Farmers turned to raising dairy cattle.

Slavery had never been allowed in Vermont. But there was a law that said escaped slaves had to be returned to their owners. Slaves who got to Canada, however, were free. Before the Civil War, many Vermont people helped slaves escape along the "Underground Railroad." It wasn't a railroad. And it wasn't underground. It was a series of houses where slaves hid on their way to Canada.

During the Civil War (1861-1865) the Northern states fought the Southern states. Vermont fought on the side of the North. Over 34,000 men from the Green Mountain State fought in the war. Over 5,000 died.

There was one unusual event in Vermont during the Civil War. Southern soldiers raided the three banks in the town of St. Albans (ALL • binz). These daring men stole $20,000. Then they escaped to Canada. One man in St. Albans had been killed. Several were wounded. This was the northernmost land fighting of the Civil War.

The North won the Civil War. After the war, cities across America grew. People from many countries came to work in Vermont factories. Lumber from Canada was sent to Burlington (BER • ling • ton) to be cut into boards. Barre (BARE • ee) became a center for mining granite. The making of guns, tools, clothing, maple syrup, and organs brought people to Vermont cities.

Rock-of-Ages quarry, Barre

Vermont produced a United States president not long after the Civil War. Chester Alan Arthur (1829-1886) was born in Fairfield. He was a schoolteacher and a lawyer. In 1855 he won a case that gave blacks the right to ride New York City streetcars. Chester Arthur was elected vice-president in 1880. When President Garfield was shot to death in 1881, Chester Arthur became the 21st president.

In the early 1900s Vermont became a big vacation state. People went there to ski. They went to see the

Skiing at Killington

Above: Chester A. Arthur home, Fairfield
Left: Street in Plymouth

historic places where the Green Mountain Boys fought
and lived.

In 1923 another Vermont man became President of the
United States. Calvin Coolidge (1872-1933) was born on
a farm at Plymouth (PLIH • mith) Notch. As a boy he
plowed fields and milked cows. He became a lawyer. He
ran for different offices, and won. In 1920 he was elected
vice-president under President Harding. On August 3,
1923 Calvin Coolidge was at his father's farm. Word
came: President Harding was dead. Calvin Coolidge's
father gave him the oath of office by the light of an oil
lamp. At 2:30 A.M. Coolidge became our 30th president.

Calvin Coolidge was a shy man, and *very* quiet. "I've made a bet that I can make you say three words," a lady once told him. "You lose," said "Silent Cal" Coolidge. He kept a lot of pets in the White House—including a raccoon. In 1924 Coolidge won election as president on his own by a huge amount.

In 1927 floods killed 60 Vermont people and wrecked towns. During World War II (1939-1945) Vermont factories made tools and weapons for the war effort.

Modern Vermont has kept many of its traditions and ways of life. It has no big cities. About two of every three Vermonters live in rural areas. Tourists still come to Vermont. But Vermonters do not want to change their state for the tourists. For instance, in 1936 Vermonters talked of building the "Green Mountain Parkway." It was to be a highway along the length of the Green Mountains. Vermonters voted it down. They didn't want to spoil the wilderness. In 1970 Vermont passed a law to protect its environment.

You have learned about some of Vermont's history. Now it is time to take a trip—in words and pictures—through the Green Mountain State.

Vermont is a small state. People have biked across Vermont in a day. Others have hiked down the whole state in a few days. Canada is to the north of Vermont. The state of New Hampshire is to the east across the Connecticut River. Massachusetts is to the south. New York is to the west. Lake Champlain, mostly in Vermont, is in the northwest. Vermont also has fewer people than most other states.

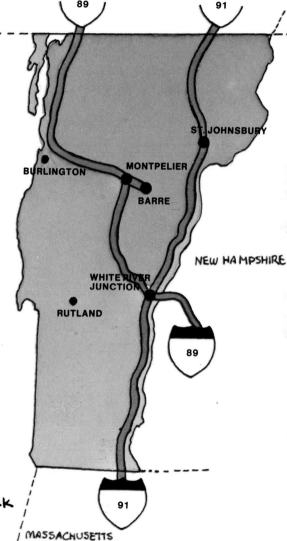

Above: Wilderness backpacking at Killington
Right: Hikers at Smuggler's Notch

The Green Mountains haven't changed much. Today,
you can walk the Long Trail which winds through the
Green Mountains. A teacher named James P. Taylor
began building this trail with a group of hikers, in 1910.
It goes through the state from Massachusetts to Canada.
Long Trail goes over 40 mountain peaks. It dips through
valleys filled with wild flowers in the spring.

In the winter, the Green Mountain State often lies
under a blanket of snow. People come to ski in the Stowe
area and at such places as Killington Peak.

Killington Gondola Tramway

Some animals are gone from the Green Mountains. There are no more wolves or catamounts (mountain lions). But there are still some bears. There are many deer. Bobcats and porcupines live in the Green Mountain National Forest and elsewhere in the state.

About three-fourths of Vermont is covered by forests. There are millions of beautiful maple trees. Some maple trees provide wood for furniture. Others provide tasty maple syrup.

Maple syrup comes from sugar maples. First, "tap holes" are drilled in the trees. In late winter and early spring, the sap begins to run. The sap is taken to a "sugarhouse" to be boiled. Once boiled, it is maple syrup. If the sap is boiled long enough, it becomes maple sugar. Vermont is the leading state for producing maple syrup—just ahead of New York.

Maple tree

Pails capture the maple sap

Cattle corn growing at Putney

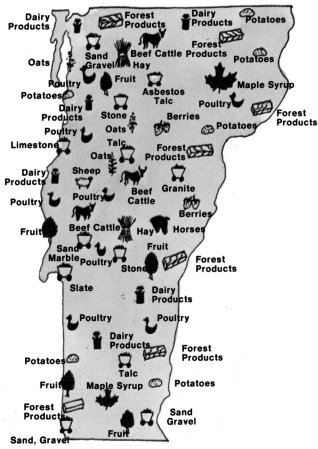

Spring planting, East Braintree

Vermont has many farms. Milk is the biggest farm product in the state. Cheese, ice cream, and other things are made from this milk.

Potatoes, apples, oats, and corn are also grown by Vermont farmers. Beef cattle, sheep, and poultry are raised by some Vermonters.

Above: Main barn, University of Vermont Morgan
Horse Farm
Left: Morgan Horse

The *Morgan horse* was bred in Vermont. About two
hundred years ago a schoolteacher named Justin Morgan
accepted a colt as payment of a debt. The colt developed
strong muscles. It was good at pulling plows. It was a
good horse for racing or riding. The children and
grandchildren of this horse came to be known as *Morgan
horses.* Morgan horses were used by the cavalry during
the Civil War. They can be found all across the country
now.

Vermont has no giant cities. Even its biggest cities have much of the feel of a small town. The towns and cities have white churches, old buildings, and lovely village greens.

The names of Vermont's cities, towns, and villages remind you of the state's history.

Places with French names: Montpelier, Vergennes (ver • GENZ), Calais (cal • LAY), Isle La Motte

Places with English names: Londonderry, Leicester (LIE • kes • ter), Westminster, Manchester, Windsor

Places with American pioneer names: Waitsfield, Jay, Irasburg, Chittenden, Enosburg, Starksboro

Burlington is Vermont's biggest city. It is on the eastern shore of Lake Champlain. The Green Mountains are to the east. Because of its beauty, Burlington is nicknamed the "Queen City of Vermont." Once, Abnaki

Church Street, Burlington

and Iroquois Indians hunted here. The city was founded in 1763. It was named after the Burling family, who owned land in the area. The Allen family played a big role in the early days of Burlington. Ira Allen built a shipyard on the Winooski (weh • NOOS • ski) River in 1772. Ethan Allen spent his last years on a nearby farm. He is buried in Burlington. "His spirit is in Vermont now," read the words on the marble cemetery statue.

Today, Burlington makes breakfast cereals, metal products, and computers. Weapons for the army are also made here.

Lake Champlain

Burlington is the home of the University of Vermont. This school was founded in 1791. The Fleming Museum is in Burlington. There you can learn about Vermont history.

You can take a boat trip on beautiful Lake Champlain. This is Vermont's biggest lake. People sail and fish on the lake that Samuel de Champlain crossed over 370 years ago.

Main Street, Montpelier

Montpelier is the capital of Vermont. Montpelier is in a valley of the Green Mountains, about 38 miles southeast of Burlington. The city lies on the Winooski River, near an old Indian trail.

The first settler in Montpelier was Colonel Jacob Davis. He built a log cabin there about 1787. The first winter, he was caught in a snowstorm and couldn't get back to his cabin. His three children survived the winter by themselves.

Montpelier was made capital in 1805 because it is near the center of the state. Under the gold dome of the State Capitol, men and women make laws for the state. The capitol building is made of Vermont granite.

Granite and plastic products are made in Montpelier. Life insurance companies make their homes there.

State House

Sidewalk art show, Barre

Barre is Vermont's fourth biggest city. It is just a few miles southeast of Montpelier.

Barre was founded in 1793. According to a story, the people had a town meeting to pick a name for their town. Two men got into a fight. The man who won named it Barre—after his hometown in Massachusetts. The first Boy Scout troop in America was formed here in 1909.

Barre is nicknamed the *Granite Center of the World.* Granite is a very hard rock. It is used to make buildings, bridges, and tombstones. Granite was formed deep under the earth, long ago. When the Green Mountains were pushed out of the earth, so was the granite. Granite is mined from deep pits, called *quarries* (KWAWR • eez). The world's largest granite quarries are in the Barre area.

Rutland is about 65 miles southwest of Barre. Rutland is Vermont's second biggest city. It is in Otter Creek Valley of the Green Mountains. The Taconic (tah • CON • ic) Mountains are to the west.

The first settlers built log cabins in Rutland in 1770. Vermont's oldest newspaper, the *Rutland Herald,* was founded in 1794. Today, scales and machinery are made here. Marble is polished in the city. People ski in the area.

One of the largest marble quarries in the United States is in Proctor, near Rutland. At the Vermont Marble Company in Proctor you can learn about this beautiful stone.

Above: Bronze statue of a catamount,
Bennington
Right: Bennington Battle Monument

Bennington is in southwest Vermont. It was named for Benning Wentworth. He was the governor of New Hampshire who granted land in Vermont. The Green Mountain Boys met at the Catamount Tavern in Bennington. A 306-foot tall monument reminds you of the Battle of Bennington (fought in New York). A famous school, Bennington College, is in North Bennington.

Brattleboro is in southeast Vermont. The English Fort Dummer was built only two miles from Brattleboro in 1724.

Places can't tell the whole story of Vermont. Many interesting people have lived in the Green Mountain State.

Robert Frost, the poet, was born in California. But he lived much of his life in Vermont. He wrote about everyday events. Three of his poems are "Birches," "After Apple-Picking," and "Stopping by Woods on a Snowy Evening."

Wilson A. Bentley (1865-1931) lived in Jericho (JAIR • i • koe). He was a farmer. He liked to study clouds, rain, and weather. He learned to photograph snowflakes. He took thousands of them. He was nicknamed "Snowflake" Bentley. The snowflakes melted long ago. But his pictures are still used.

Thomas Davenport was born in Williamstown in 1802. He was a blacksmith. But he liked to tinker with electricity. In 1834 he invented the first electric motor at his Brandon blacksmith shop. Davenport also made a small electric train and an electric piano.

Many inventors have lived in Vermont. About 1814 James Wilson of Bradford built the first world globe made in the United States. Silas Herring of Salisbury (SALZ • bury) built the first burglar-proof safe. Thaddeus (THAD • ee • us) Fairbanks of St. Johnsbury invented the platform scale in 1830.

Admiral George Dewey was born in Montpelier. He became a Navy hero during the Spanish-American War.

Zerah Colburn (ZAIR • ah COAL • burn) could multiply big numbers in his head. "What is 15 x 9?" his father would ask. Zerah had the answer in seconds. He traveled around the world to show people his skill. And he was only six years old!

Much is known about early Vermont, thanks to Abby Hemenway of Ludlow. She went across the state asking people to write down what they knew about their towns. She put the story of Vermont together—in 6,000 pages! She was in the middle of writing another book about Vermont when she died in 1890.

East
Braintree

Home to Ethan Allen ... Calvin Coolidge ... and "Snowflake" Bentley...

Producer of granite ... marble ... milk ... and maple syrup...

Land of the Green Mountains ... lovely valleys ... and beautiful Lake Champlain...

Historic towns like Bennington ... Burlington ... and Barre... covered bridges ... the Morgan horse ... skiing ... hiking...

This is Vermont—the Green Mountain State.

Facts About VERMONT

Area—9,609 square miles (43rd biggest state)

Greatest Distance North to South—155 miles

Greatest Distance East to West—90 miles

Highest Point—4,393 feet above sea level (Mount Mansfield)

Lowest Point—95 feet above sea level (Lake Champlain)

Hottest Recorded Temperature—105° (at Vernon on the 4th of July, 1911)

Coldest Recorded Temperature—Minus 50° (at Bloomfield on December 30, 1933)

Statehood—the 14th state, on March 4, 1791

Capital—Montpelier

Counties—14

U.S. Senators—2

U.S. Representatives—1

Electoral Votes—3

State Senators—30

State Representatives—150

State Songs—"Hail, Vermont!" by Josephine Hovey Perry

State Motto— *Vermont, Freedom and Unity*

Nicknames—Green Mountain State

Origin of Name Vermont—From *Vert Mont*, French for *Green Mountain*

State Seal—Adopted in 1779

State Flag—Adopted in 1923

State Flower—Red clover

State Bird—Hermit thrush

State Tree—Sugar maple

State Animal—Morgan horse

Coat of Arms Motto—Freedom and Unity

Some Colleges and Universities—Bennington College, Middlebury College, University of Vermont

Principal Rivers—Otter Creek, Winooski, Lamoille, White, Missisquoi, Mad, Ottauquechee

Largest Lake—Lake Champlain (partly in Canada and New York)

Farm Products—Milk, maple syrup, maple sugar, potatoes, apples, corn, oats, hay, beef cattle, sheep, eggs, poultry

Fishing—Perch, trout, catfish, carp, salmon, bass

Animal Life—Deer, bears, raccoons, squirrels, beavers, moose, skunks, porcupines, coyotes, otters, woodchucks, and various turtles, snakes, and birds

Manufacturing—Machines, tools, scales, computers, ski equipment, weapons, printed materials, paper products, wood products, stone products

Mining—Granite, marble, asbestos, slate, limestone, talc

Population—1980 census: 511,456 (1991 estimate: 566,000)

Major Cities	1980 Census	1990 Estimate
Burlington	37,712	39,047
Rutland	18,436	18,469
Brattleboro	11,886	13,356
South Burlington	10,679	not available
Barre	9,824	9,971
Montpelier	8,241	8,344

Where People Live—66.2 per cent in rural areas

33.8 per cent in urban areas

Vermont History

There were people in Vermont at least 10,000 years ago

About 1300-1750 A.D.—Algonquin and Iroquois Indians use Vermont for their hunting grounds

1564—An Englishman named Johne Graye possibly explores Vermont

1609—Samuel de Champlain is first explorer known to enter Vermont

1666—French build fort and shrine in Isle La Motte

1690—French build a fort at Chimney Point

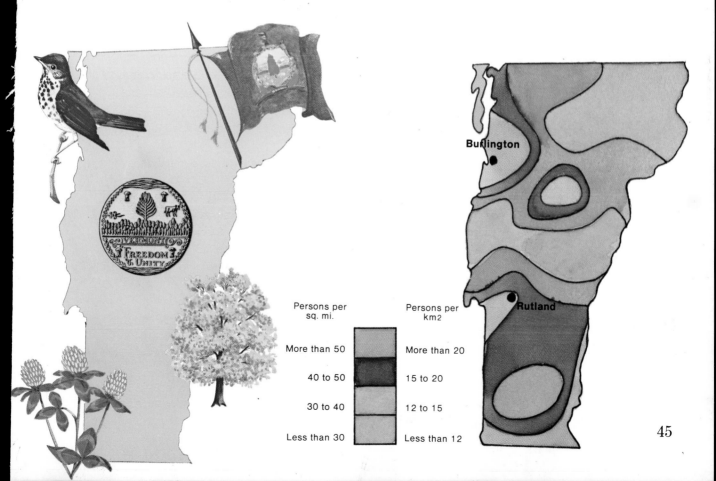

Burlington

Rutland

Persons per sq. mi.	Persons per km2
More than 50	More than 20
40 to 50	15 to 20
30 to 40	12 to 15
Less than 30	Less than 12

45

1724—First permanent settlement, Fort Dummer, is built by English near Brattleboro

1749—Governor Benning Wentworth of New Hampshire grants lands in Vermont

1754—"Captive" Johnson is born

1759—Rogers' Rangers kill 200 St. Francis Indians during French and Indian War

1760—There are 300 settlers in Vermont

1761—Settlers are coming to Bennington and other New Hampshire Grants

1763—English win French and Indian War and claim Vermont

1764—King of England says that New York owns the land

1770-1771—Ethan Allen leads Green Mountain Boys in fight against "Yorkers"

1775—Beginning of Revolutionary War; Ethan Allen captures Fort Ticonderoga on May 10; on May 12 Seth Warner takes English fort at Crown Point

1777—Vermont becomes an independent republic and Dr. Thomas Young suggests name *Vermont*

1777—The Battle of Hubbardton is fought on July 7 and the Battle of Bennington on August 16

1783—Americans have won Revolutionary War; United States of America has been born

1789—Ethan Allen dies in Burlington

1790—Argument with New York is settled for $30,000

1790—85,425 settlers live in Vermont

1791—Vermont becomes our 14th state on March 4

1794—The Rutland *Herald,* state's oldest newspaper, is established

1800—Population is 154,396

1805—Montpelier becomes capital

1812—Vermonters fight British at Chippewa, Lundy's Lane, and Plattsburg

1816—The cold, snowy "Year Without a Summer"

1823—The Champlain Canal opens and goods can travel directly by water from Vermont to New York

1829—Our 21st President, Chester A. Arthur, is born at Fairfield

1834—Electric motor is invented by Thomas Davenport, at Brandon

1840—Sheep-raising flourished in Vermont

1848—Railroad in Vermont

1861—Civil War begins; 34,328 Vermont men fight for Union

1864—Southern soldiers raid banks at St. Albans

1865—Civil War ends

1872—Our 30th President, Calvin Coolidge, is born at Plymouth Notch

1881—Chester Arthur becomes President

1891—Happy 100th birthday, Green Mountain State!

1900—Population is 343,641

1910—Long Trail is begun through Green Mountains

1914-1918—During World War I, about 16,000 Vermont men and women
serve in the armed forces

1923—Calvin Coolidge becomes President

1927—Vermont's worst flood in history kills 60 and destroy towns

1929—Lake Champlain bridge opens at Chimney Point

1934—First ski tow in U.S. is built at Woodstock

1939-1945—World War II, 49,942 Vermont men and women serve

1954—Consuelo N. Bailey is elected first woman Lieutenant Governor in U.S.

1960—Population of Green Mountain State is 389,881

1970—Vermont lawmakers pass Environmental Control Law

1985—Madeleine Kunin becomes first woman governor of Vermont

1989—Governor Kunin signs a law restricting toxic emissions from autos and
light trucks beginning with 1993 models

1991—Richard A. Snelling is elected governor.

INDEX

47

INDEX, Cont'd.

About the Author:

Dennis Fradin attended Northwestern University on a creative writing scholarship and was graduated in 1967. While still at Northwestern, he published his first stories in *Ingenue* magazine and also won a prize in *Seventeen's* short story competition. A prolific writer, Dennis Fradin has been regularly publishing stories in such diverse places as *The Saturday Evening Post, Scholastic, National Humane Review, Midwest,* and *The Teaching Paper*. He has also scripted several educational films. Since 1970 he has taught second grade reading in a Chicago school—a rewarding job, which, the author says, "provides a captive audience on whom I test my children's stories." Married and the father of three children, Dennis Fradin spends his free time with his family or playing a myriad of sports and games with this childhood chums.

About the Artists:

Len Meents studied painting and drawing at Southern Illinois University and after graduation in 1969 he moved to Chicago. Mr. Meents works full time as a painter and illustrator. He and his wife and child currently make their home in LaGrange, Illinois.

Richard Wahl, graduate of the Art Center College of Design in Los Angeles, has illustrated a number of magazine articles and booklets. He is a skilled artist and photographer who advocates realistic interpretations of his subjects. He lives with his wife and two sons in Libertyville, Illinois.